THE BEST
JOKE
...with elephant
and pickle jokes
BOOK
for kids

THE BEST JOKE BOOK

...with elephant
and pickle jokes

for kids

compiled, collected, and
laughed over by the kids of
JOAN ECKSTEIN and **JOYCE GLEIT**
illustrations by
JOYCE BEHR

AN AVON CAMELOT BOOK

THE BEST JOKE BOOK FOR KIDS is an original publication of Avon Books. This work has never before appeared in book form.

Cover Design by Little Apple Art.

AVON BOOKS
A division of
The Hearst Corporation
1790 Broadway
New York, New York 10019
Copyright © 1977 by Joan Eckstein and Joyce Gleit
Published by arrangement with the authors.
Library of Congress Catalog Card Number: 77-78096
ISBN: 0-380-01734-2

Book Design by Lucille Salvino

First Camelot Printing, October, 1977

CAMELOT TRADEMARK REG. U.S. PAT. OFF. AND IN
OTHER COUNTRIES, MARCA REGISTRADA, HECHO EN
U.S.A.

Printed in the U.S.A.

BAN   20   19   18   17   16   15   14   13   12

INTRODUCTION

These are the jokes, kids. They were collected, laughed over, told and retold a million times by our own kids, Jonathan, Stephanie, Lisa and Paul, and their many giggling friends.

What kind of watch does a
ghost like best?

A death-watch.

What does a ghost do to relax?

He takes a five minute coffin
break.

How does a ghost eat?

By goblin.

What did one ghost say to the other?

Do you believe in people?

How do ghosts pass through a locked door?

They have a skeleton key.

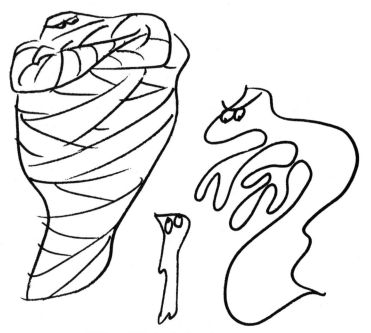

What did the baby ghost say to
the bully ghost?

Leave me alone or I'll tell
my mummy.

What do ghosts eat for breakfast?

Ghost toasties.

What did the witch say to the
baby ghost?

Fasten your sheet belt.

4

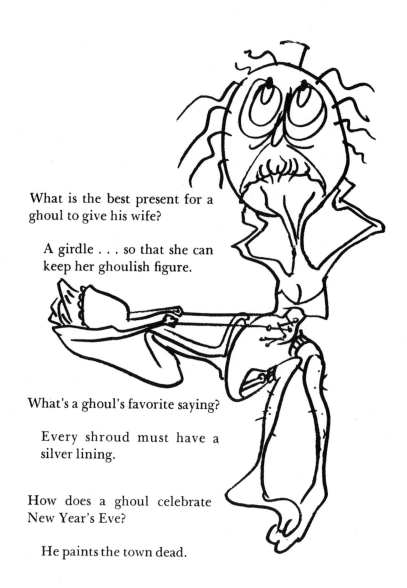

What is the best present for a ghoul to give his wife?

A girdle . . . so that she can keep her ghoulish figure.

What's a ghoul's favorite saying?

Every shroud must have a silver lining.

How does a ghoul celebrate New Year's Eve?

He paints the town dead.

When does a ghoul wear denims?

When they are tie-died.

What is the favorite song of our monster friends?

"The Ghoul That I Marry."

Why do so many ghouls spend their time at the cemetery?

Because people are dying to get in.

What did the ghoul do when he saw the funeral procession?

He took a turn for the hearse.

Why do witches fly on brooms?

Because vacuum cleaners are too expensive.

Why don't monsters make good dancers?

Because they have three left feet.

How does a ghoul start a letter?

Tomb it may concern.

What is a vampire's favorite tourist place?

The Vampire State Building.

How do you call a monster?

From very far away.

Why does a ghoul hang around
the coroner?

The morgue the merrier.

What holiday is the best of all?

April Ghoul's Day.

What do they scream at a
Transylvanian baseball game?

Kill the Vampire! Kill the
Vampire!

Why didn't the skeleton cross
the road?

Because he didn't have the guts.

What could a monster eat after
it had its teeth pulled?

Its dentist.

What sort of beans does a
werewolf like best?

Human beans.

What do you call a clean, neat,
hard working, kind, intelligent
monster?

A failure.

What do you call a monster that is ten feet tall, has five arms and poisonous fingernails?

Sir!

Where do baby monsters come from?

Frankenstorks.

What do you have when you cross a drip-dry shirt with a monster?

A wash-and-wear wolf.

What's the favorite dish of our fiendish monster?

Hungarian Ghoulash.

Mother Cannibal to Witch Doctor: "I'm worried about Junior, he wants to be a vegetarian."

PATIENT: "Doctor, that ointment you gave me makes my arm smart."

DOCTOR: "In that case, rub some on your head."

PATIENT TO PSYCHIATRIST: "Help me, Doctor. I can't remember anything for more than a few minutes. It's driving me crazy."

DOCTOR: "How long has this been going on?"

PATIENT: "How long has what been going on?"

PATIENT: "Are you sure I'll get well? I've heard doctors sometimes give wrong diagnoses, and treat patients for pneumonia who later die of typhoid fever."

DOCTOR: "Don't worry, when I treat a man for pneumonia, he dies of pneumonia."

DENTIST: "What kind of filling do you want in your tooth?"

JONATHAN: "How about chocolate or marshmallow?"

FATHER: "Doctor, you have to help me. My son thinks he's a chicken."

PSYCHIATRIST: "How long has this been going on?"

FATHER: "About five years now."

PSYCHIATRIST: "Why did you wait so long to bring him in?"

FATHER: "Well, we needed the eggs."

PATIENT: "Doctor, when I get well will I be able to play the piano?"

DOCTOR: "Of course."

PATIENT: "That's marvelous. I never played it before."

FOOTBALL PLAYER: "Coach, can I have three thousand dollars to go to a movie?"

COACH: "Three thousand dollars to see a movie! Are you crazy?"

PLAYER: "No coach. It's a drive-in and I don't have a car."

What makes the floors of a basketball court all wet?

The players . . . they dribble a lot.

What would you say to the hockey player that earns $250,000 a year?

That's ice work if you can get it.

How do the players keep cool at a basketball game?

There are lots of fans there.

How did the athlete sprain himself at the Olympics?

By slipping his discus.

When do the Siamese twins
love baseball best?

When it's a double-header.

How did the midget qualify for
the basketball team?

He lied about his height.

A proud father was bragging about his son, a great all-around athlete but a little dim in the classroom. "My son won his fourth letter this winter," he boasted to a friend.

"That's good," replied the other, "but I bet you had to read it to him."

How do you fit six elephants in a Volkswagen?

Two in the front, two in the back and two in the glove compartment.

What did the telephone company say to the elephant?

"Stop using your own trunk line!"

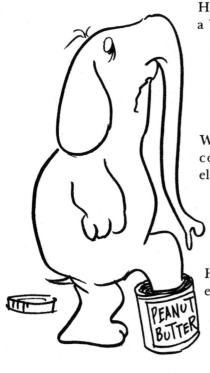

How can you tell if there's an elephant in your refrigerator?

By the footprints in the peanut butter.

How do you get down off an elephant?

You don't get down off an elephant, you get down off a duck.

How do you stop a herd of elephants from charging?

You take away their credit cards.

What's grey inside and clear outside?

An elephant in a baggie.

What time is it when an elephant sits on a fence?

Time to get a new fence.

A huge elephant and a tiny mouse were in the same cage at the zoo. The elephant looked down at the mouse and nastily trumpeted in disgust, "You're the puniest, the weakest, the most insignficant thing I've ever seen!"

"Well," squeaked the mouse, "don't forget, I've been sick."

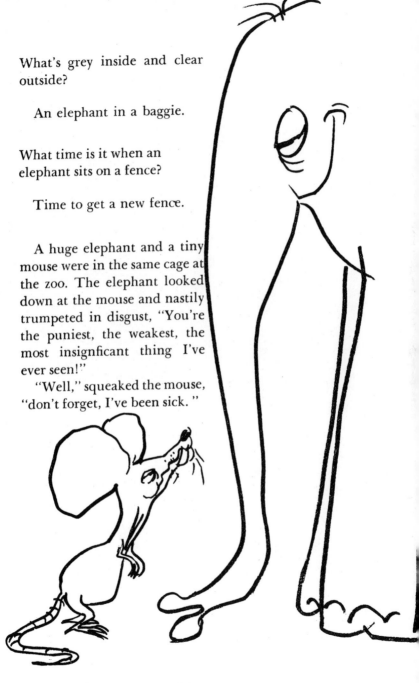

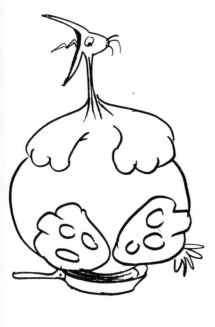

Why do elephants make such good piano players?

They love to tickle the ivories.

What do you get if you cross a chicken with an elephant?

I don't know, but Colonel Saunders would have a lot of trouble trying to dip it into the batter.

How do you catch an elephant?

You hide in the grass and make a noise like a peanut.

How do you make an elephant stew?

You keep it waiting for a few hours.

What do you get when you cross a parrot with an elephant?

An animal that tells what it remembers.

What would you do if an elephant sat in front of you at the movies?

Miss most of the movie.

What do you feed a stampeding elephant?

Anything it wants.

Why will an elephant work for low wages?

Because he loves to work for peanuts.

PAUL: "Today I saw a baby that gained ten pounds in two weeks by drinking elephant's milk."

JON: "You don't say! Whose baby was it?"

PAUL: "The elephant's."

What was the elephant doing on Route 325?

About four miles per hour.

Why do so many elephants wear bright green nail polish?

So they can hide in the pea patch.

How can you trail an elephant in the jungle?

By the slight smell of peanuts on its breath.

TEACHER: "Willy! Can you tell me the capital of Alaska?"

WILLY: "No'm."

TEACHER: "That's right."

SUNDAY SCHOOL TEACHER: "Willy! Can you tell me who built the ark?"

WILLY: "Naw."

TEACHER: "That's right."

TEACHER: "What is the difference between electricity and lightning?"

PUPIL: "We don't have to pay for lightning."

TEACHER: "Randy, if you put your hand in one pants pocket and you find 75¢ and you put your hand in the other pants pocket and find 25¢, what would you have?"

RANDY: "I'd have somebody else's pants on!"

The absentminded teacher said, "I have brought in a frog for the class to study." With that the teacher carefully unwrapped the package he was carrying. Inside was a neatly wrapped ham sandwich. "That's odd," he said, "I distinctly remember having eaten my lunch."

TEACHER: "How many sexes are there?"

SAMMY: "Three."

TEACHER: "Three! Can you name them?"

SAMMY: "Male sex, female sex and insects."

STUDENT: "But I don't think I deserve a zero on this exam."

TEACHER: "Neither do I, but it's the lowest mark I can give you."

TEACHER: "Name five things that contain milk."

BARRY: "Butter, cheese, ice cream and two cows."

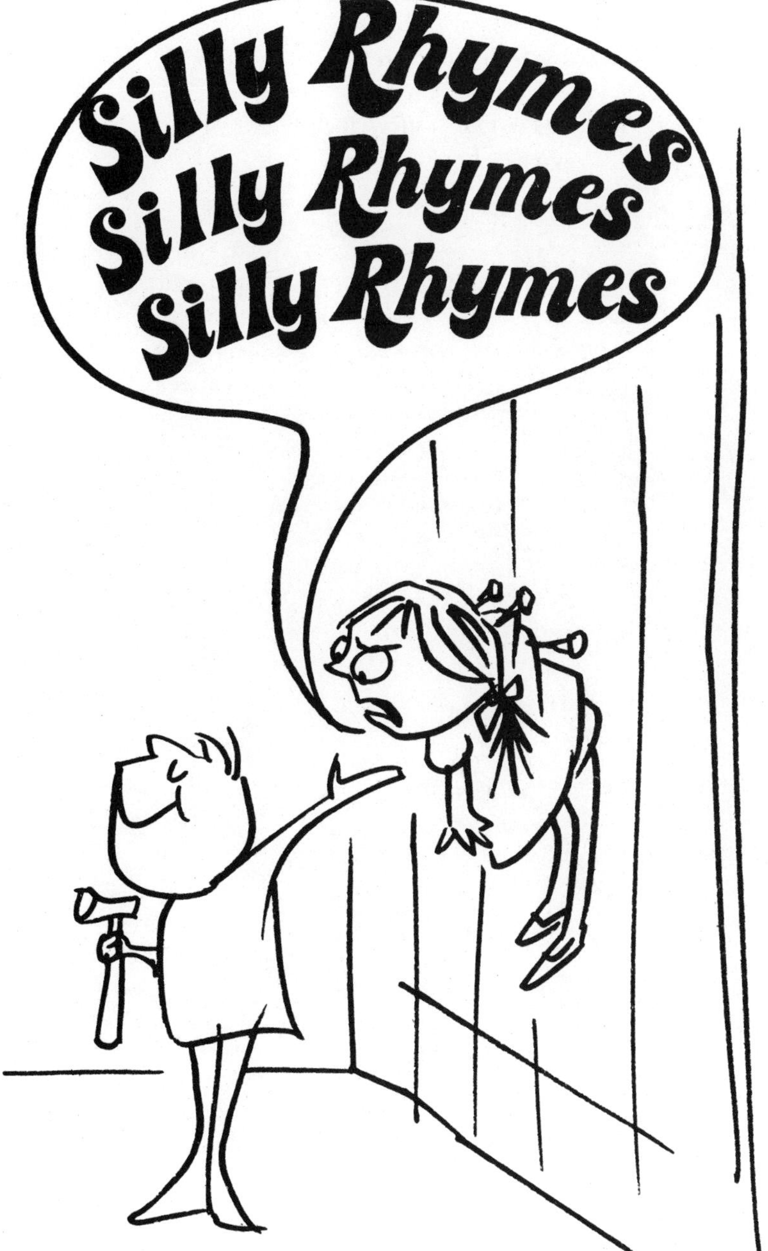

Willie, with a thirst for gore,
Nailed his sister to the door.
Mother said, with humor quaint:
"Now, Willie dear, don't scratch the paint."

A peanut sat on a railroad track;
His heart was all-a-flutter.
A train came speeding down the track.
Toot! Toot! Peanut Butter.

Cathy had a little car
And it was painted red.
And everywhere that Cathy went
The cops picked up the dead.

Mary had a little lamb
And tied him to a heater.
And every time he turned around
He burned his little seater.

A little green vampire, in his green little way
Some little green apples devoured one day;
And the little green grasses now tenderly wave
O'er the little green vampire's green little grave.

Early in the morning in the middle of the night
Two dead boys got up to fight
Back to back they faced each other
Drew their swords and killed each other
A deaf policeman heard the noise
And came and killed the two dead boys.

Hickory dickory dock
The mice ran up the clock
The clock struck one—
And the others escaped with minor injuries.

As I was standing in the street,
As quiet as could be,
A great big ugly man came up
And tied his horse to me.

It was midnight on the ocean
Not a streetcar was in sight.
The sun was shining brightly
And it rained all day that night.
A barefoot boy with shoes on
Stood sitting on the grass
A bumblebee flew by and the streetcar stopped to let it
    pass.

Be kind to your web-footed friends
For a duck may be somebody's mother.
It lives in the fields and the swamp
Where the weather is very damp.
Now you may feel that this is the end—
Well it is!

What kind of shoes are made
out of banana skins?

Slippers.

What does the garden say when
it laughs?

Hoe, hoe, hoe.

What is the worst weather for
rats and mice?

When it rains cats and dogs.

What is the most difficult key
to turn?

A donkey.

What do turtles give each
other?

People-neck sweaters.

What's green and crawly and
has 100 legs?

A centipickle.

What word is usually
pronounced wrong, even
by the best of scholars?

"Wrong", of course.

Why does a dog wag its tail?

Because no one else will wag
it for him.

What did Paul Revere say
when he finished his famous
ride?

Whoa.

If you put three ducks into a
crate, what would you have?

A box of quackers.

What did the judge say when
the skunk came into the court-
room?

Odor in the court.

What's a twip?

It's when a wabbit wides on a
twain.

What happened when the canary flew into the blender?

Shredded tweet.

What has four legs and flies?

A picnic table.

Why couldn't anyone play cards on Noah's Ark?

Because Noah was always standing on the deck.

What keeps the moon from falling?

Its beams, of course.

If that's a watchdog, how come he's running around in circles?

Because he's all wound up.

Why do giraffes have such long necks?

Because their heads are so far away from their bodies.

Where does a jellyfish get its jelly?

From ocean currents.

Why do spiders spin webs?

They don't know how to knit.

Why did the girl put her bed in the fireplace?

Because she wanted to sleep like a log.

If a King sits on Gold, who sits on Silver?

The Lone Ranger.

What American has had the largest family?

George Washington. He was the father of our country.

Did you take a bath?

No. Is one missing?

HAPPY FATHER'S DAY

What is never of any use unless it is in a tight place?

A cork.

Why does a cow wear a bell?

Because its horns don't work.

Why do they have mirrors on chewing gum machines?

So you can see how mad you look when the gum doesn't come out.

What's faster than a speeding bullet, more powerful than a locomotive and green?

Superpickle.

Why are the Middle Ages called the Dark Ages?

Because there were so many knights in them.

Do you know that there is a pickle growing out of your ear?

What? I planted corn.

What's hard and green and writes under water?

A ball-point pickle.

What's green and wears a mask and rides silver?

The Lone Pickle.

Why did the chicken cross the road?

To lay it on the line.

What is orange and half a mile high?

The Empire State Carrot.

How many big men have been born in California?

None. Only babies.

How do you make an apple turnover?

Tickle it in the ribs.

If athletes have athlete's foot, what do astronauts have?

Missile toes.

What is purple and 5,000 miles long?

The Grape Wall of China.

What is a history of cars called?

An autobiography.

Why did the rooster refuse to fight?

Because it was a chicken.

What is the best thing to take when you are run down?

The number of the car that hit you.

What did one billy goat say to the other?

Eaten any good books lately?

What happens if you cross a parrot with a gorilla?

When Polly wants a cracker, he gets it—fast!

What goes through a door, but
never goes in or comes out?

A keyhole.

Where was the Declaration of
Independence signed?

At the bottom.

What is black and wrinkled
and makes pit stops?

A racing prune.

To what man does everyone
always take off his hat?

The barber.

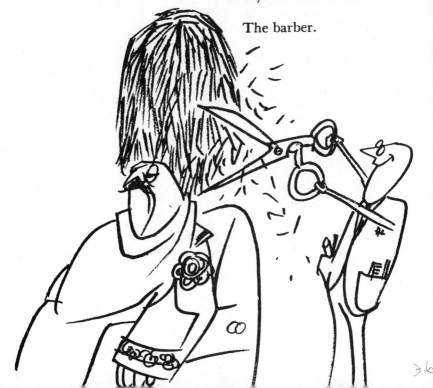

36

BOY: "Here comes the parade now. Judy will miss it if she doesn't come to the window. Where is she?"

GIRL: "She's upstairs waving her hair."

BOY: "For Pete's sake, hasn't she got a flag?"

HOLDUP MAN (pointing a gun at movie cashier): "The picture is terrible. Gimme everybody's money back."

SUSIE: "Mommy, the boy next door broke my doll."

MOM: "That's too bad, dear. How did he do it?"

SUSIE: "I hit him over the head with it."

BOY: "The laundry made a mistake and sent me the wrong shirt. The collar is so tight I can hardly breathe."

GIRL: "That's your shirt all right. You've got your head through the buttonhole."

BOSS: "Didn't I tell you to notice when the glue boiled over?"

WORKER: "I did, it was a quarter past ten."

BOY: "How come you're wearing your socks inside out?"

GIRL: "Because there's a hole on the outside."

BOY: "I found a horseshoe."

GIRL: "Do you know what that means?"

BOY: "Sure. Some horse is running around in his bare feet."

MOTHER: "Well, Tommy, how did you get along with your father while I was away?"

TOMMY: "Just fine. Every morning he took me down to the lake in the boat and let me swim back."

MOTHER: "My, that's a long swim, isn't it?"

TOMMY: "I made it all right. The only trouble I had was getting out of the bag."

PAUL (In a restaurant): "Go see if the chef has pig's feet."

JON: "I can't tell. He has his shoes on."

BOY: "Why did you cut a hole in your umbrella?"

GIRL: "So I could tell when it stops raining."

CUSTOMER: "Waiter! What is this fly doing in my soup?"

WAITER: "It looks like the backstroke to me."

MOTHER CANNIBAL TO CHILD: "How many times have I told you not to speak with someone in your mouth?"

CALLER: "Weather Bureau?"

WEATHER BUREAU: "Yes."

CALLER: "How are chances for a shower tonight?"

WEATHER BUREAU: "O.K. by me. Take one if you need it."

DOPEY CITY KID: "Why does cream cost more than milk?"
DOPEY COUNTRY BOY: "Because it's harder for the cows to sit on the small bottles."

A man was seated in the movie house with his arm around a large dog sitting in the seat next to him. The dog was clearly enjoying the picture and even yelped at the funny parts. A man sitting behind them leaned over and said, "Pardon me, sir, but I can't get over your dog's behavior."

The man turned around and said, "Frankly it surprises me too. He hated the book."

ROBBER: "This is a holdup. Give me your money or else."
VICTIM: "Or else what?"
ROBBER: "Don't confuse me. This is my first job."

A man and a dog were sitting at a table playing chess. A lady walked by and almost fainted. "Why, that's the most amazing thing I ever saw," she said.

"What's so wonderful," barked the dog. "I haven't won a game yet."

EXPLORER TO EDUCATED CANNIBAL: "Do you mean to say that you went to college and you still eat your enemies?"
CANNIBAL: "Yes, but of course now I use a knife and fork."

The house painter was on a ladder and his partner was down below. "Have you got a good firm grip on the brush?" yelled the one down below.

"Yep," the one above called.

"O.K. then hang on. I need the ladder."